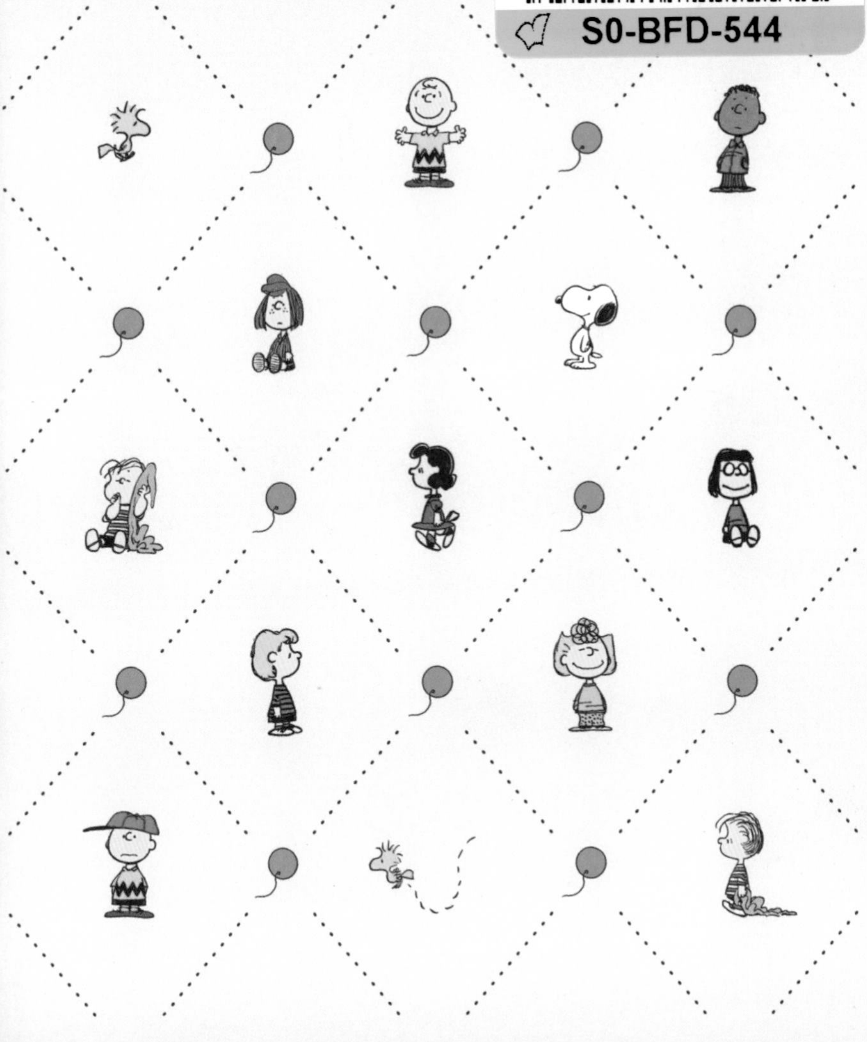

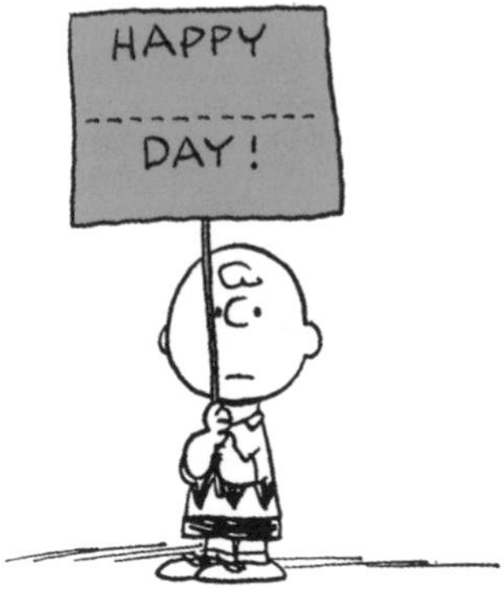
HAPPY
DAY!

Published in Great Britain in 2015 by Canongate Books Ltd,
14 High Street, Edinburgh EH1 1TE

canongate.co.uk

4

British Library Cataloguing-in-Publication Data
A catalogue record for this book is available on
request from the British Library

ISBN 978 1 78211 365 2

PEANUTS written and drawn by Charles M. Schulz
Edited by Jenny Lord and Andy Miller
Design: Rafaela Romaya
Layout: Stuart Polson

Printed and bound in the UK by Bell and Bain Ltd

CHARLES M. SCHULZ

THE PEANUTS GUIDE TO
HAPPINESS

CANONGATE

IT'S TOO HARD
TO FEEL SORRY
FOR YOURSELF
WHEN YOU'RE
HAPPY

HAPPY BEETHOVEN'S BIRTHDAY!
I BROUGHT YOU A LITTLE PRESENT...

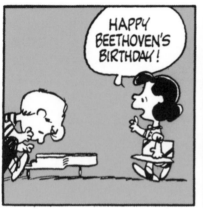

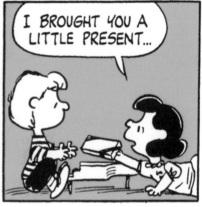

WELL, THANK YOU...JUST WHAT I'VE ALWAYS WANTED
ELTON JOHN GLASSES!

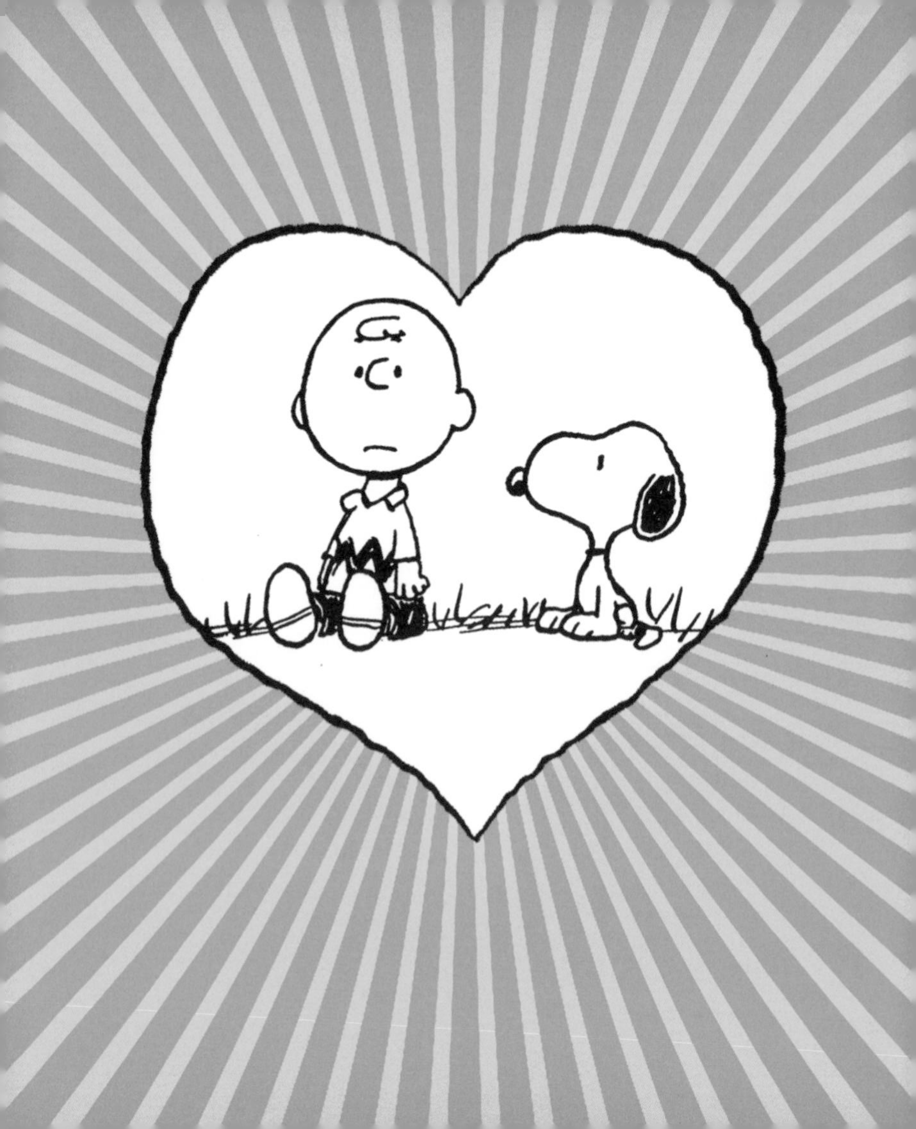

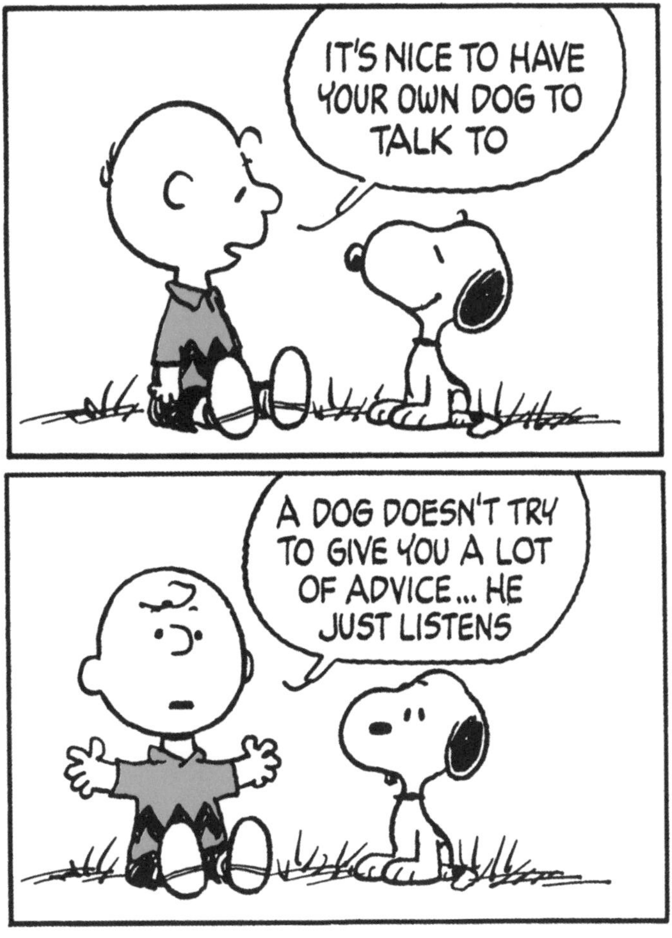
IT'S NICE TO HAVE YOUR OWN DOG TO TALK TO
A DOG DOESN'T TRY TO GIVE YOU A LOT OF ADVICE... HE JUST LISTENS

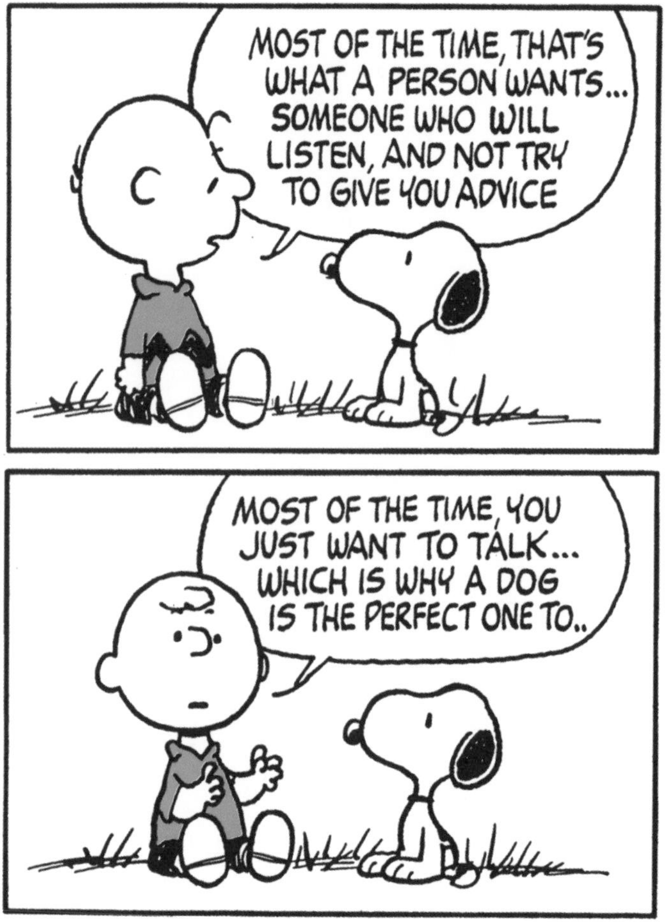
MOST OF THE TIME, THAT'S WHAT A PERSON WANTS... SOMEONE WHO WILL LISTEN, AND NOT TRY TO GIVE YOU ADVICE
MOST OF THE TIME, YOU JUST WANT TO TALK... WHICH IS WHY A DOG IS THE PERFECT ONE TO..

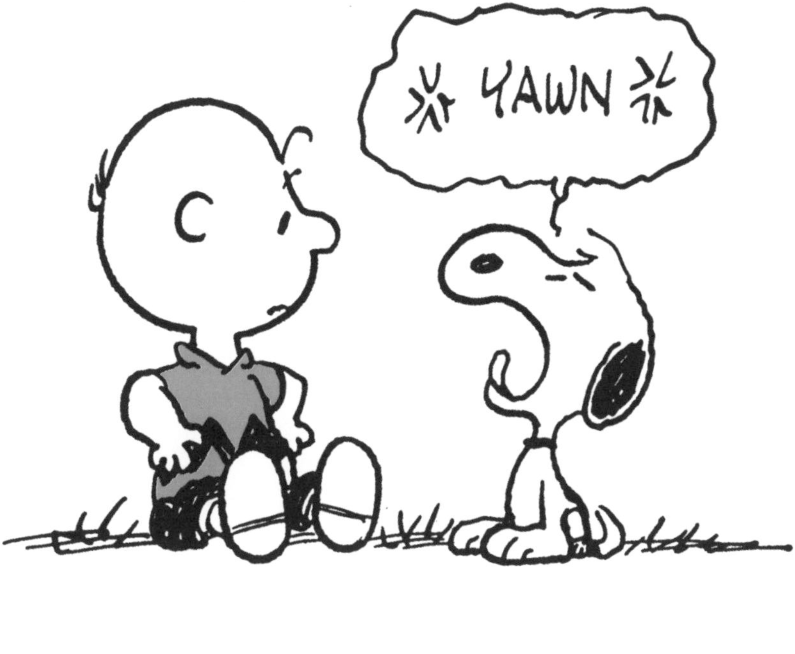
YAWN

WHAP!
I LOVE RAKING!

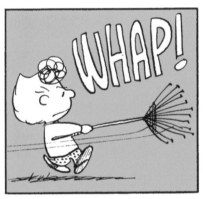

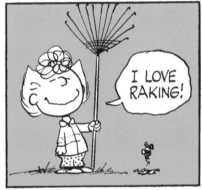

LAUGHING IS
GOOD FOR YOU...
IF YOU DON'T
KILL YOURSELF

SCHOOL IS OUT!
NO MORE SCHOOL! SCHOOL IS OUT!!

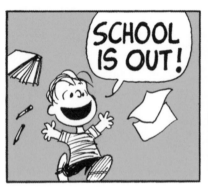

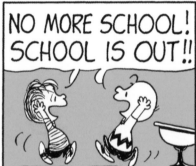

ALL RIGHT, EVERYONE OVER HERE FOR THE CAMP BUS! IN YOU GO! HURRY IT UP! EVERYONE TO SUMMER CAMP!
WHATEVER HAPPENED TO GOING HOME?

DO YOU THINK THAT LIFE HAS ITS PEAKS AND VALLEYS?
YES, I'M SURE THAT IT HAS
THEN, THAT MEANS THAT THERE MUST BE ONE DAY ABOVE ALL OTHERS IN EACH LIFE THAT IS THE HAPPIEST, RIGHT?

YES, I GUESS THAT'S PROBABLY TRUE...
WHAT IF YOU'VE ALREADY HAD IT?

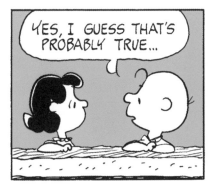

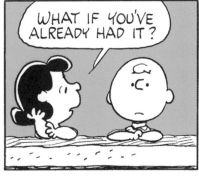

TO DANCE
IS TO LIVE!

SMAK!
OLD MOVIES SORT OF AFFECT ME THAT WAY..

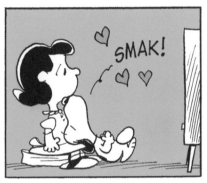

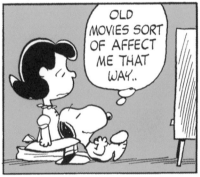

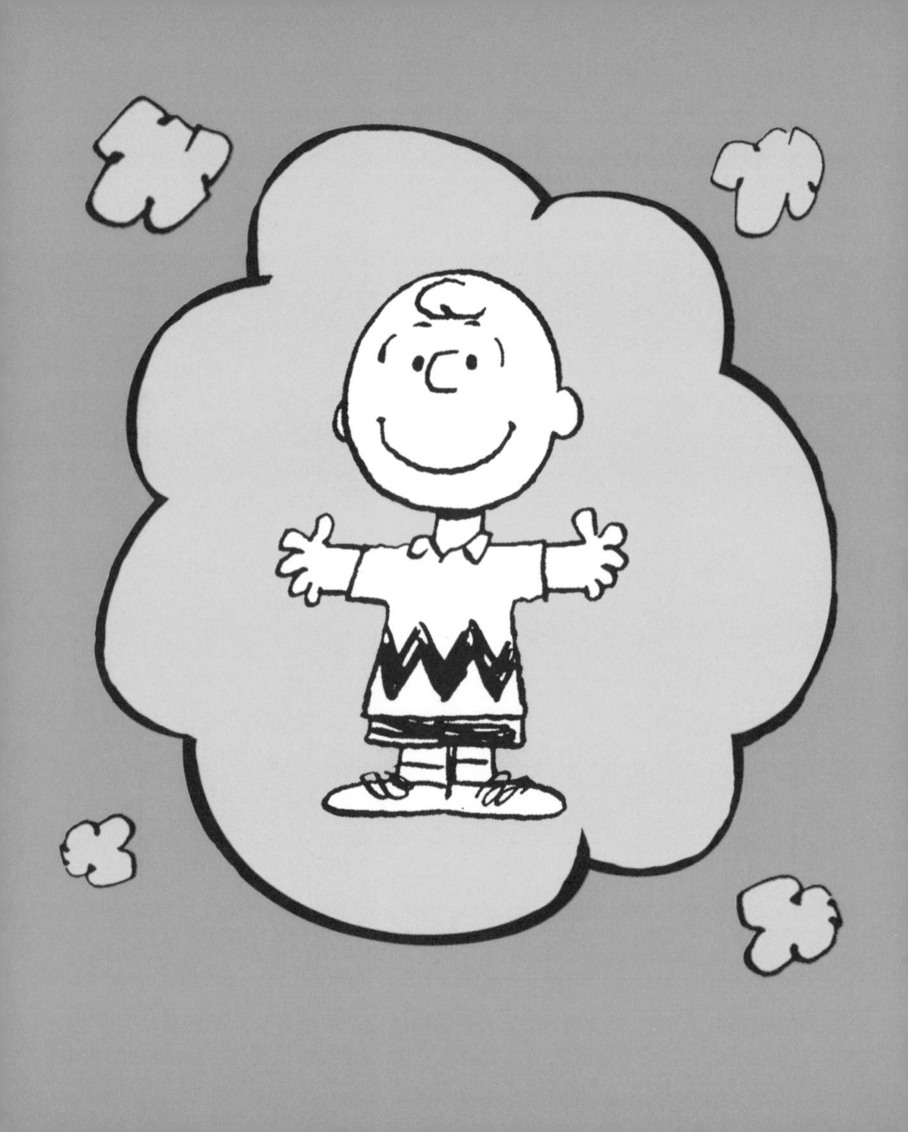

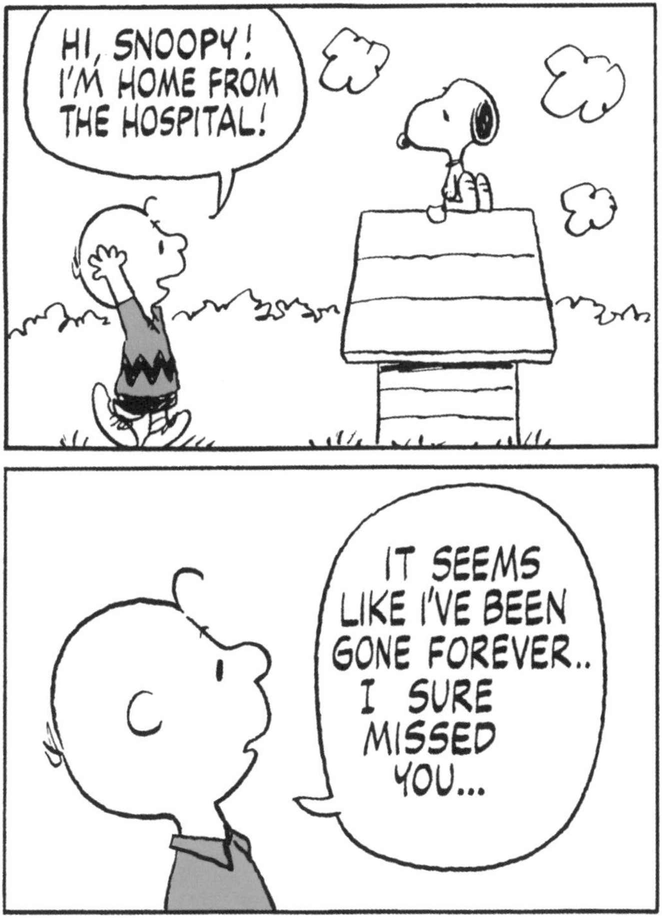
HI, SNOOPY! I'M HOME FROM THE HOSPITAL!
IT SEEMS LIKE I'VE BEEN GONE FOREVER.. I SURE MISSED YOU...

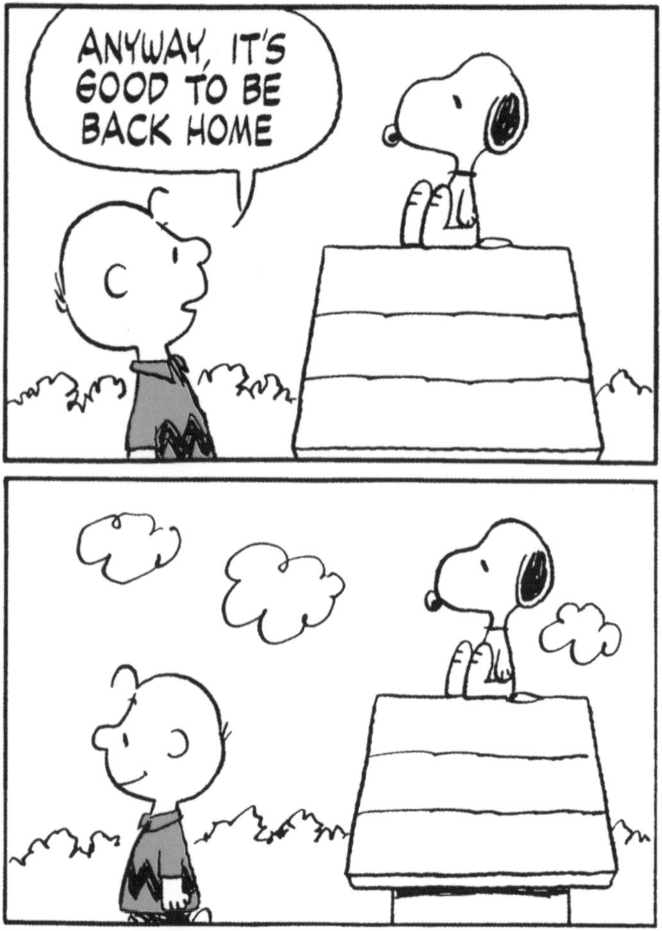
ANYWAY, IT'S GOOD TO BE BACK HOME

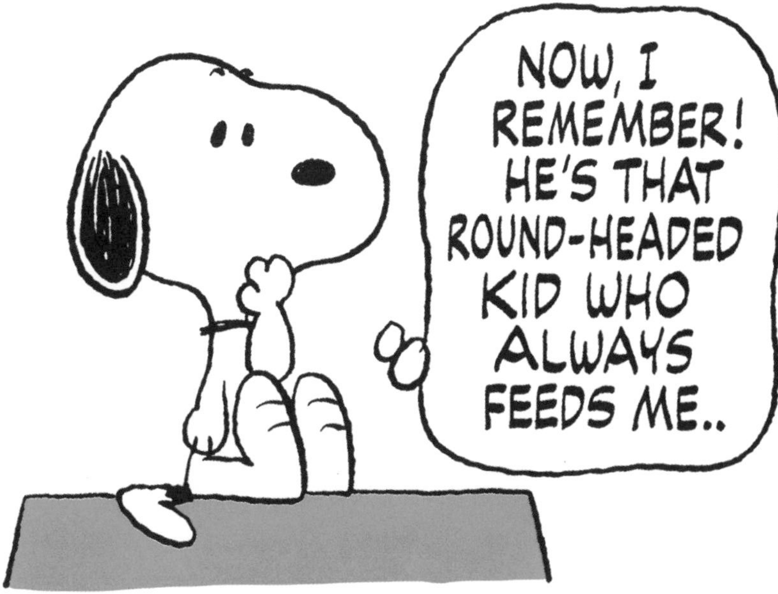
NOW, I REMEMBER! HE'S THAT ROUND-HEADED KID WHO ALWAYS FEEDS ME..

I GOT SIX COMPLIMENTS TODAY...
FANTASTIC!

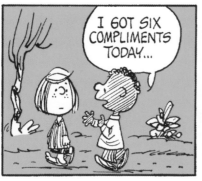

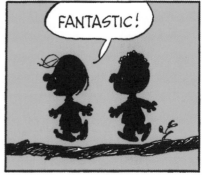

IT'S NOT OFTEN YOU CAN GET SIX COMPLIMENTS IN ONE DAY
TWO OF THEM WERE EVEN SINCERE!

IT'S IMPOSSIBLE TO BE GLOOMY WHEN YOU'RE SITTING BEHIND A MARSHMALLOW

I GOT AN "A" ON MY REPORT, SNOOPY!
BECAUSE YOU WERE SUCH A BIG HELP, I'M GOING TO TREAT YOU TO AN ICE-CREAM CONE

FORTY-NINE FLAVORS
YOU WEREN'T THAT BIG A HELP!

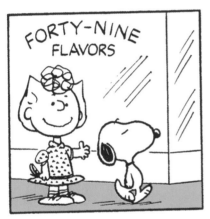

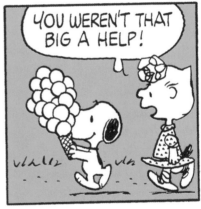

YOU THINK YOU'D BE HAPPY IF YOU WON A BALL GAME, DON'T YOU, CHARLIE BROWN?
THE DOCTOR IS IN
WELL, YOU WOULDN'T! IF YOU WON ONE GAME, YOU'D WANT TO WIN ANOTHER, AND THEN ANOTHER!

SOON YOU'D WANT TO WIN EVERY BALL GAME YOU PLAYED...
YEAHHH!!

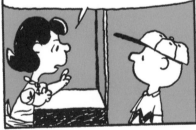

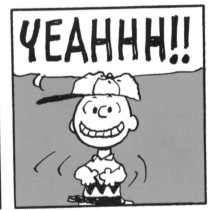

A NEW YEAR'S TOAST!
TO THAT WONDERFUL GENIUS...

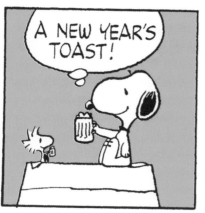

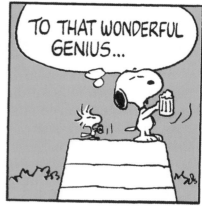

TO THAT PERSON WE ALL ADMIRE...
THE INVENTOR OF THE DOGGIE BAG!

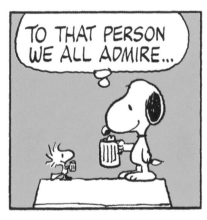

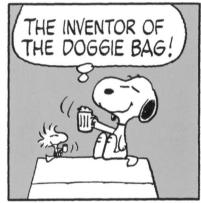

HAPPINESS SHOULD BE SHARED

STAND REAL STILL AND FEEL THE WARM SUN ON YOUR BACK...

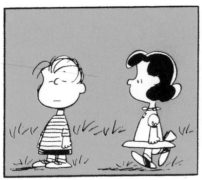

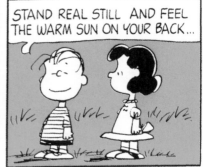

DOESN'T THAT FEEL GREAT?
AND IT'S FREE

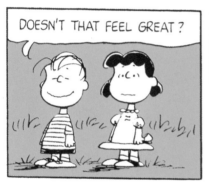

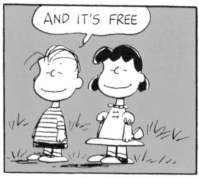

LUDWIG VAN BEAGLE!

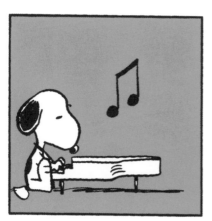

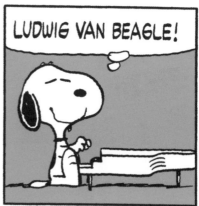

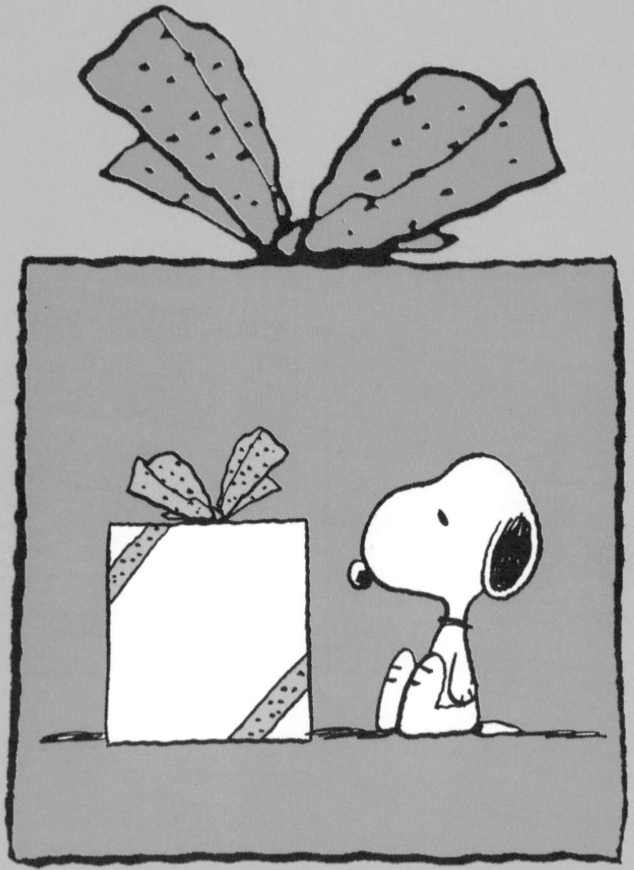

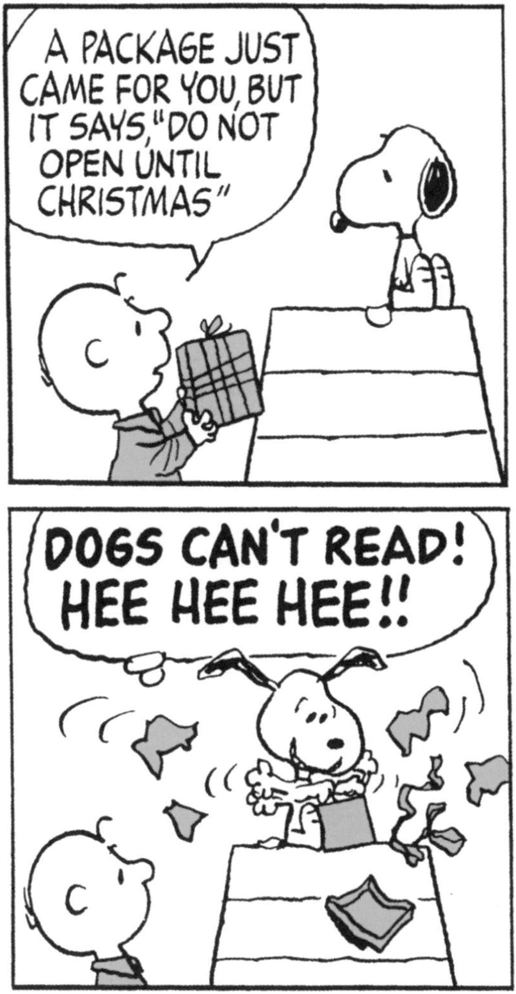
A PACKAGE JUST CAME FOR YOU, BUT IT SAYS, "DO NOT OPEN UNTIL CHRISTMAS"
DOGS CAN'T READ! HEE HEE HEE!!

YOU WON!
CONGRATULATIONS! I CAN'T BELIEVE IT!

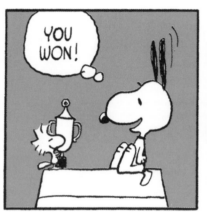

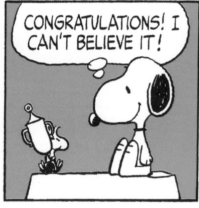

LET ME SEE WHAT IT SAYS ON THE TROPHY..
HOW ABOUT THAT? "MOST IMPROVED BIRD"

SOMETIMES I
LOVE LIFE SO
MUCH I CAN'T
EXPRESS IT

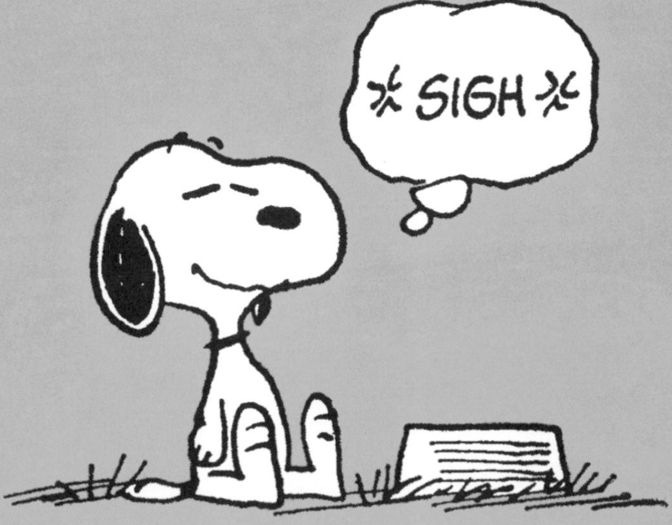
SIGH

LOOK, BIG BROTHER!
THEY ACCEPTED MY APPLICATION NOT TO GO TO CAMP! HOW ABOUT THAT!

BOY, AM I EVER **LUCKY**!!
NOW, I CAN HANG AROUND THE HOUSE ALL SUMMER AND DETERIORATE!

MAYBE YOUR SONGS AREN'T HAPPY ENOUGH
AFTER ALL, IT'S SPRING!

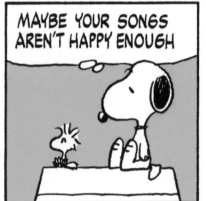

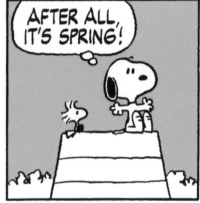

SING SOMETHING THAT MAKES PEOPLE HAPPY...

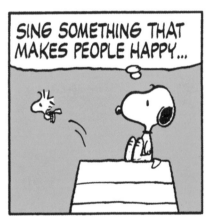

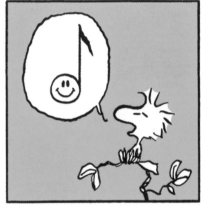

A SMILE EACH DAY WILL BRING HAPPINESS YOUR WAY

TODAY IS THE TWO HUNDREDTH ANNIVERSARY OF THE BIRTH OF BEETHOVEN...
I SHALL CELEBRATE IT BY GIVING YOU A KISS ON THE NOSE!
HOW QUAINT..

THE KISS WILL BE SUPPLIED BY MY REPRESENTATIVE..
SMAK
AAAUGHH!
HAPPY BEETHOVEN'S BIRTHDAY!

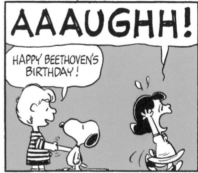

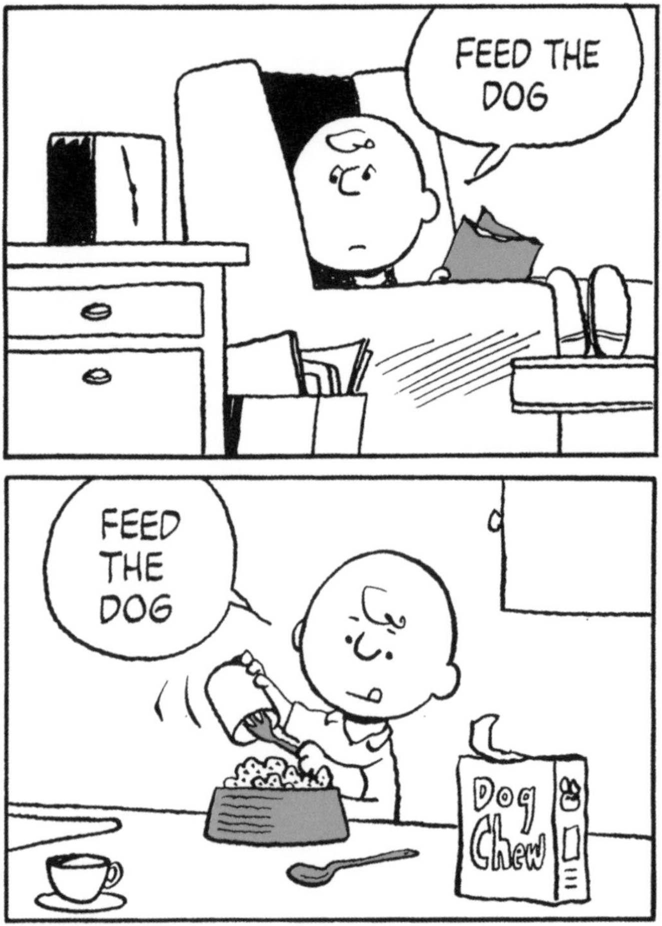
FEED THE DOG
FEED THE DOG
Dog Chew

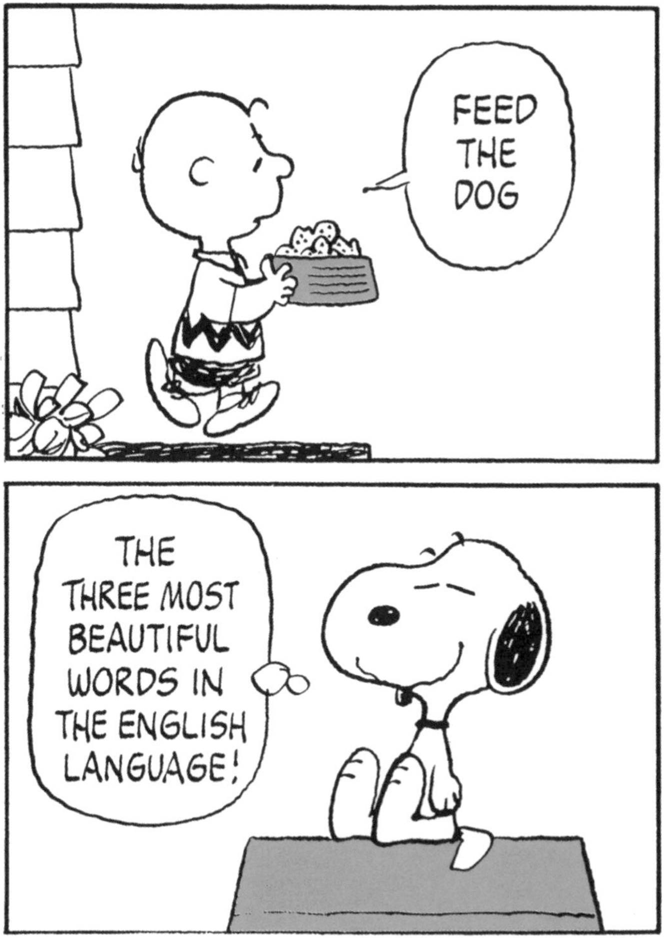
FEED THE DOG
THE THREE MOST BEAUTIFUL WORDS IN THE ENGLISH LANGUAGE!

CHOMP
CHOMP
CHOMP

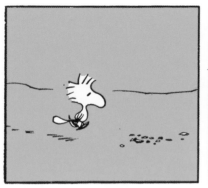

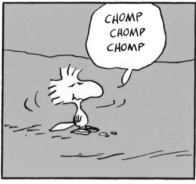

WOODSTOCK IS THE ONLY PERSON I KNOW WHO CAN BLOW HIS MIND ON BREAD CRUMBS...

HAPPINESS
IS A
WARM PUPPY

aaaaaaaa
bbbbbbbbbb
A'S AND B'S ARE BORING...

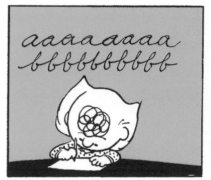

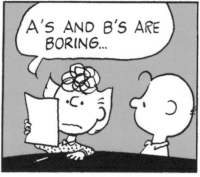

E'S ARE FUN!

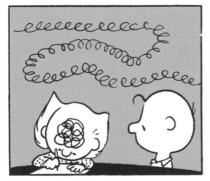

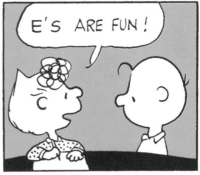

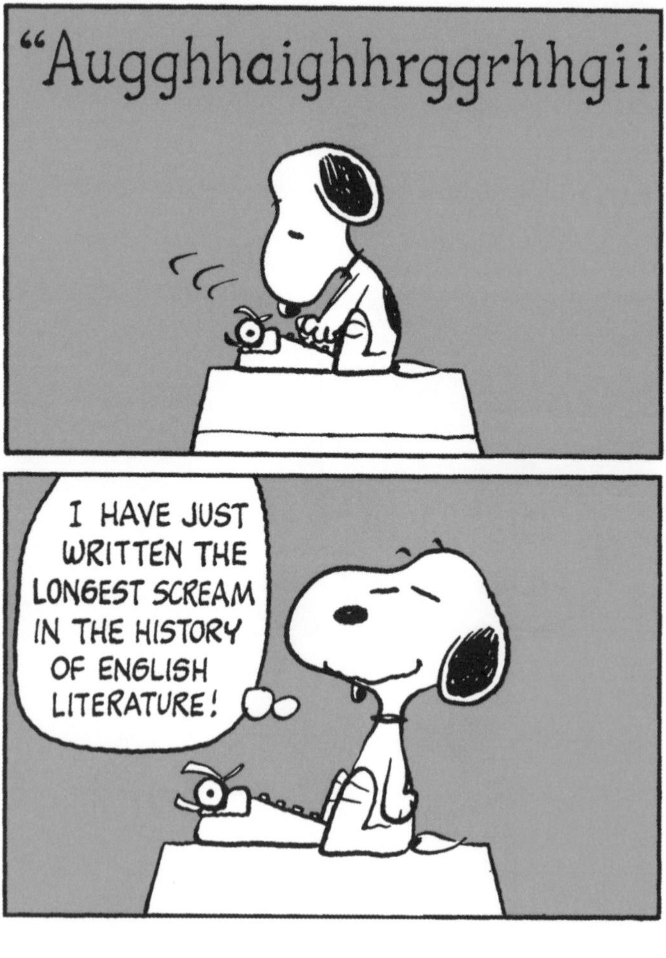
"Augghhaighhrggrhhgii
I HAVE JUST WRITTEN THE LONGEST SCREAM IN THE HISTORY OF ENGLISH LITERATURE!

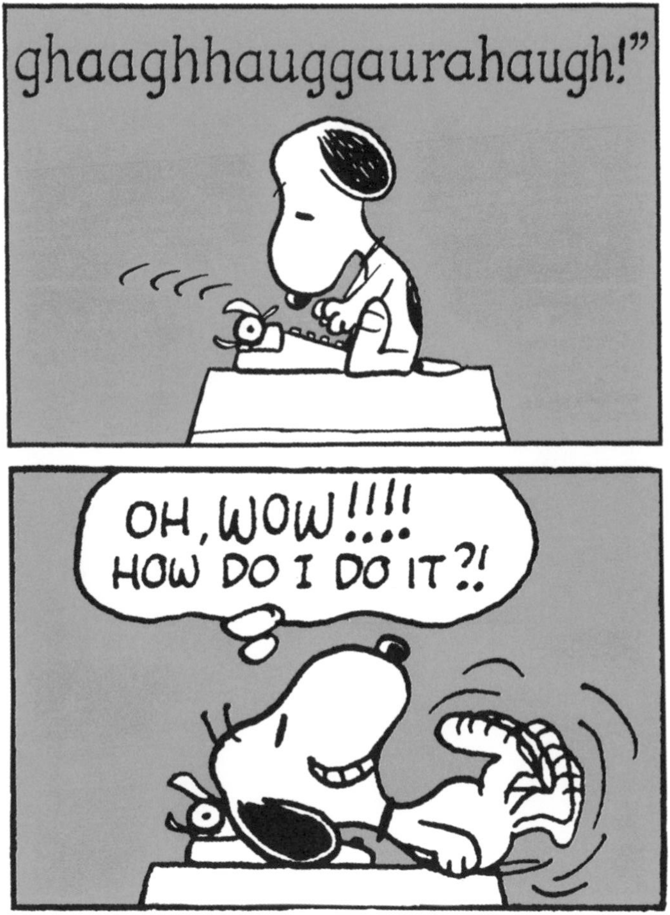
ghaaghhauggaurahaugh!"
OH, WOW!!!!.... HOW DO I DO IT?!

IT DOESN'T TAKE MUCH TO MAKE HIM HAPPY...

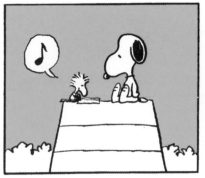

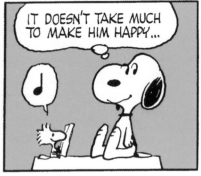

I LET HIM PUT IN ALL THE BLUE SKIES IN MY COLORING BOOK

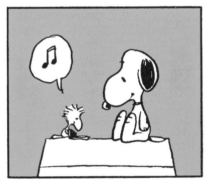

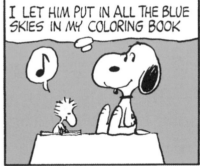

HAVE YOU EVER KNOWN ANYONE WHO WAS HAPPY?

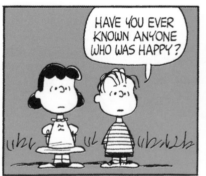

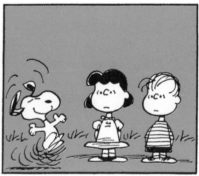

SMAK
AND WAS STILL IN HIS RIGHT MIND, I MEAN..

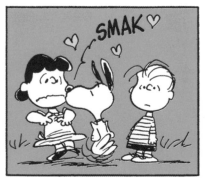

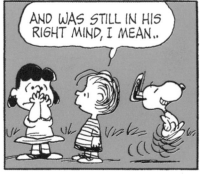

YOU KNOW
WHO I WANT
TO BE LIKE
WHEN I
GROW UP?
ME!

??????
MY HANDS AREN'T SHAKING ??!!??
I'M NOT DIZZY ANY MORE... MY STOMACH DOESN'T HURT.. I'M ACTUALLY HUNGRY!

I MADE IT THROUGH THE WEEKEND WITHOUT MY BLANKET! I DID IT! I DID IT!
AND I DID IT MY WAY!!

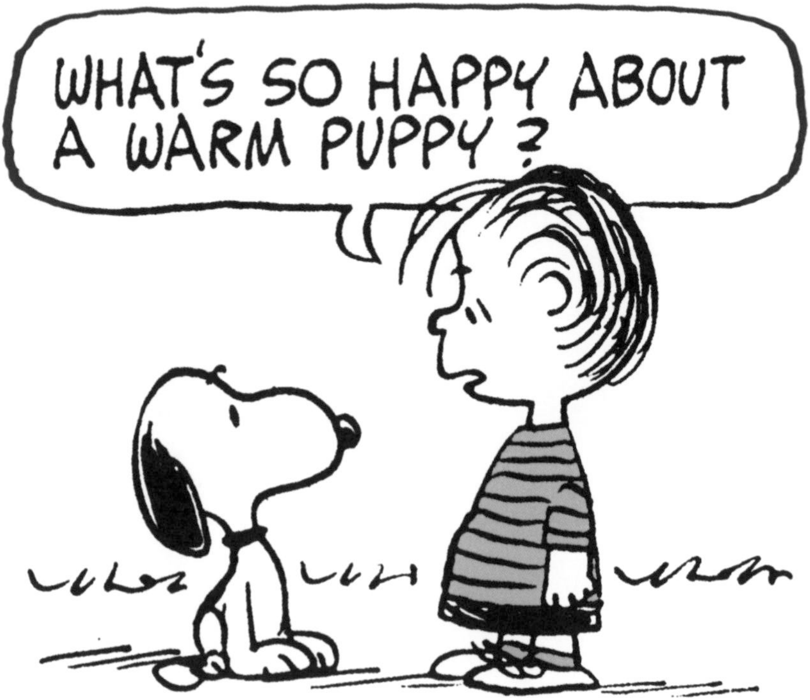
WHAT'S SO HAPPY ABOUT A WARM PUPPY ?

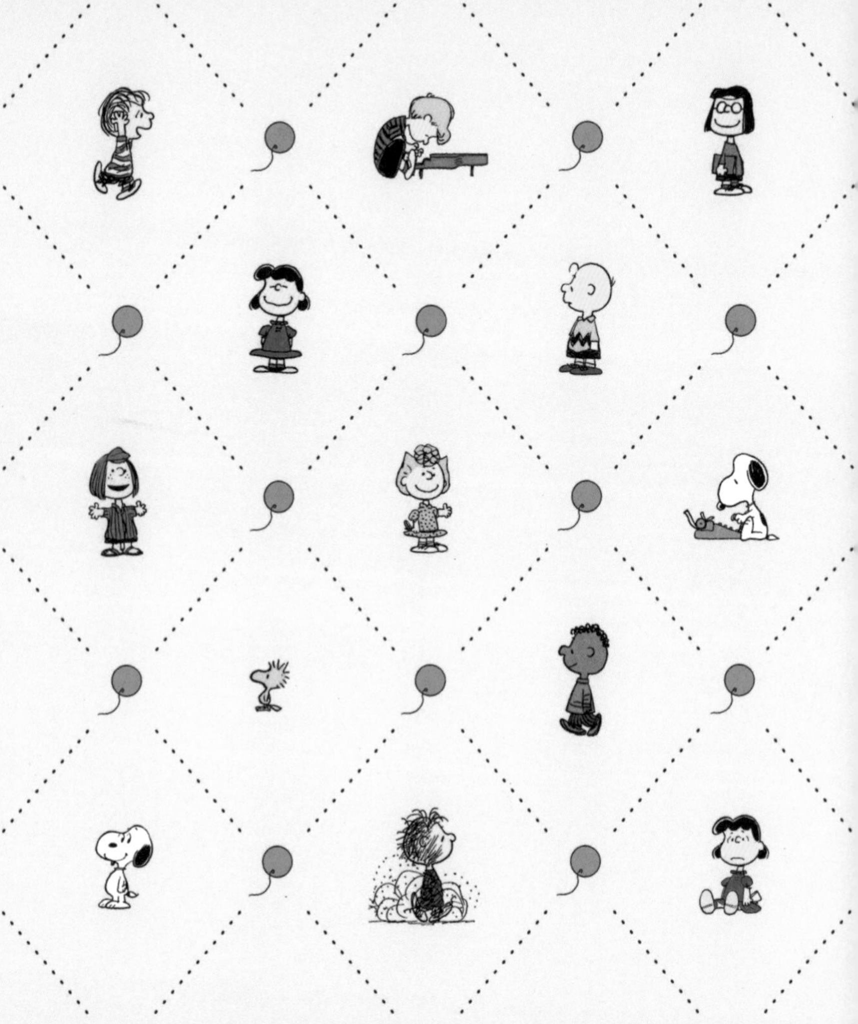